POUNDCAKE &
Private Practice

5 Things I Learned During My First Year

CRYSTAL JOSEPH, CCM, LCPC, LPC

PsycYourMind Consulting, LLC

POUNDCAKE & PRIVATE PRACTICE
Published by PsycYourMind Consulting, LLC
Copyright © 2018 Crystal Joseph, CCM, LCPC, LPC

Printed in the United States of America
ISBN-10: 978-0-692-05043-9

Unless otherwise, indicated, al scripture quotations are taken from the Message Remix: The Bible in Contemporary Language, copyright © 2003. Used by permission of Nav-Press Publishing Group, Permissions, P.O. Box 35001, Colorado Springs, CO 80395.

Cover photo by Tyrone Singletary and Shane Redman of R|S Wedding Photography
Special Thanks to Sarah Kosterlitz
Cover design by Nicole Miller
Edited by Joylynn Ross of End of the Rainbow Projects

Books may be purchased by contacting the publisher and author at
www.PoundCakeandPrivatePractice.com

POUNDCAKE &
Private Practice

5 Things I Learned During My First Year

CRYSTAL JOSEPH, CCM, LCPC, LPC

Contents

"But because God was so gracious, so very generous, here I am. And I'm not about to let his grace go to waste. Haven't I worked hard trying to do more than any of the others? Even then, my work didn't amount to all that much. It was God giving me the work to do, God giving me the energy to do it. So whether you heard it from me or from those others, it's all the same: We spoke God's truth and you entrusted your lives." **I Corinthians 15:10-11 MSG**

To the $19 that wasn't enough.

Introduction

As my one-year business anniversary approached, I sat down to explore the idea of writing about my experiences while building PsycYourMind, my very own psychotherapeutic, private practice. During Summer 2015, I decided to jump off a cliff—backward and blindfolded—into the waters below. Oh, and did I mention I can't swim? This choice was a lifeline for me, reflecting an intrinsic value to serve those who lack agency, people who look like me, and be a beacon of light for those who wish to do better with their education and training. I have served those in palaces and those without homes. Some days I feel as if I have seen it all, and other days like my favorite color, green.

A true cook knows not everyone's recipe is appealing to his or her own palette. Thus, this book will reflect my experiences, and is not meant to serve as an immediate replication of a private practice; but rather, provide and express the level of tenacity, wherewithal, and pragmatism of maintaining one's integrity and economy in this industry. Thank you in advance for reading.

For those who do not know, pound cake is equal parts

or equal weight of five major ingredients: flour, eggs, butter, sugar, and vanilla—with several variations at the discretion of the preparer. My great-grandmother's pound cake is quite dense. Only a chosen few family members can finish the entire two-inch slice during holidays.

I chose this word-phrase to magnify the proposed equal weight I garnered in order to succeed during my first year of private practice. From cover to cover, I will share my five major ingredients.

I had several restless nights in May 2015. For me, this was odd. I love sleep. Sleep is non-negotiable. No, I cannot be bribed. For my job function, I need all of my synapses firing off at the proper speed. My clients are amused at the details I remember on a week-to-week basis. Sleep is my magic. Eventually, I realized I was being disturbed by God.

"Wake up, Crystal."

After three consecutive sleepless nights, I grabbed a scraggly sheet of paper and traced out what is now my company logo. I toyed with several color options, deciding on orange for charisma and blue for trust or fidelity. I wanted the "POW!" effect from the old Batman show. Revamp how people think about counseling and therapy. Get in their faces a bit. Okay, great, I have a logo . . . now what?

During this time, I was a resident in counseling, losing my sparkle. This was not due to lack of recognition. I was lauded by my residency clinical director as the "best employee she had." I received her hand-me-down clients that did not fit into her schedule. In previous years, my internship clinical supervisor chuckled during one of our one-on-one supervision meetings, exclaiming, "Man, you could do circles around some of the psychologists I know!" Yet and still, these patented statements did nothing for the vacuum that was growing inside of me.

My best friends and family will tell you that I have always wanted to be a therapist. I even took my intro to psych courses in high school, which would later transfer as college credit. So, what was the problem? To add a linear quality to my story, for most people in my field, residency is equivalent to the second-to-last rung on a ladder. The top of the ladder is licensure—clinical independence.

During this multi-thousand-hour experience, clinical expertise is sharpened, and real-life scenarios play out in ways that make you want to burn your textbooks Waiting to Exhale Bernadine style. Eight years prior to my residency, I had been in possibly every job setting in the mental health field. From being chased down Georgia Avenue by a client while attempting to employ the interventions of Assertive Community Treatment, to managing a medical intermediate care facility, to having boardroom discussions with investors as a subject matter expert, I've seen and done it all. Then it dawned on me; I was being shaped. Placed in the not-so-great job functions with the not-so-great supervisors in order to: 1) discover the cracks in the system, and 2) correct the errors in my own system.

I am grateful for all my experiences, so I don't want people to get this twisted. Just keep in mind the vision—your vision—at all times. It seemed I had lost sight of mine during the final stages of my clinical training.

Now let me discuss the characteristics of flour for a bit. You know someone is throwing down in the kitchen when they have flour on their nose, forehead, elbows, and feet. Seriously, how can one begin to contain the small particles of flour? It gets everywhere! Flour is the base for many confections, gravies, and coatings for meat. It stands as the tabula rasa for your culinary imagination. To my point . . . if flour is not properly seasoned, cut into, kneaded, or contained, it will go where the air carries it. Your vision must not be carried away from you, cut into, rolled into itself, or seasoned by anyone other than you. Your vision is the blank slate for you to adorn. It will serve as the foundation for larger ideas to come.

In my initial excitement regarding the inception of Psy-cYourMind, I wanted to tell the world, but I knew better (side-eye). From previous experience, I learned you cannot tell everyone what you are birthing and expect them to align with that idea. I received support from my family and closest friends. I then decided to test the waters—let me probe others in the field who look like me, and who are doing this on a daily basis. By "this," I mean running a successful, minori-ty-owned business while jumping through legal, ethical, and financial hoops that are ablaze.

Did you know (here comes the researcher in me) only four percent of licensed mental health professionals in the United States are Black? I know a handful, and until recently, that only meant one hand. I ran my vision by the first person—a psychologist. Anyone ever experience hot tears and a tight throat? Yeah, that was me. It was not what she said, per se, but the fact that she could not believe in my vision when she herself was doing what I hoped to do. Was that conversation even real? I had to walk around the parking lot to get myself together before my next session.

That evening, my mother reminded me, in Angela

Davis-fashion, what I presented was not this woman's vision, but solely my own. She also told me to be prepared for the naysayers, I-wish-I-knew-that-when-I-was-your-age-types, and wolves in sheep's clothing. But maybe the psychologist was right? All I had was my vision . . . oh yeah, and the logo.

Remember, flour cannot stand alone . . .

XIII

1

This is YOUR Vision
Flour

Business Structure/Business Plan

I had the privilege of working for an investor as a case manager and research coordinator, serving as a subject matter expert for a projected white paper. My tenure was under auspicious pretenses, as a company merger was ominous. I was previously housed in a private, successful case management firm in which the owner wished to sell. After the merger, my tenure shifted to tenuous, but more on that in chapter five.

During this time, I was a part of many Knights of the Round Table (which was actually square) meetings. Board-room presentations and pitches were held at least weekly, as an idea for a successful business operation grew.

In these hour-long meetings, I learned the importance of several mantras. One—*this* is no one else's dream but your own. "This" is defined as your vision. While you may ask another's opinion, at the end of the day, you *can* and *will* do what you wish with your vision. Two—don't waste your time explaining yourself or apologizing. I am laughing as I write this, because I witnessed and was the recipient of blunt interruptions by the investor. Did he apologize to those he cut off? Absolutely not! Where his deferent behaviors may be deemed rude in colloquial conversation, (t)his behavior was expected in the board room. Some days, I would hold my breath, counting the seconds that passed as someone's words would be severed from their lips before reverberating through the air.

Mantra number three—speak up for yourself and your vision. Day after day, week after week, I watched him interrupt others—myself included. I made sure to meet his fervor with my own. (Flips hair.)

In order for the investor to receive any monetary consideration from future stakeholders, a business structure and business plan was defined, redefined, and reiterated on almost a daily basis. A business plan is a living document, in my opinion. The business plan lights the way for yourself and others you may wish to include on your journey.

The states I practice in do not require a business plan to be submitted in conjunction with the articles of organization application. Yet, some of the verbiage required on the application came directly from my business plan. Consult an attorney on how you wish to "incorporate" your business. Also, see the resource appendix for more information on how to differentiate between business suffixes.

My use of the word "incorporate" is not to state one must have an INC. at the end of their business name. There are multiple options for suffixes in relation to the business structure type. If you look me up, I am a Limited Liability Company with the suffix LLC operating as a sole proprietor. This means if someone were to sue me, they cannot come for me like the Wicked Witch of the West—"you and your little dog too." Lyric will be safe and sound as the pampered pooch that she is.

Business Structure vs. Tax Classification

I was confused about business structure and tax classification until my husband showed me in an architecture module. Better late than never, right? I know my paperwork is correct—I'm still in business! I will try my best to explain the two.

As mentioned earlier, there are multiple ways to incorporate. Here is a non-exhaustive list that varies by state:

> Sole Proprietorship
> Limited Partnership
> Limited Liability Partnership (LLP)
> Corporation
> Nonprofit Corporation
> Limited Liability Company (LLC)

When I applied for my LLC, Virginia State Corporation Commission required I select a business structure type; I chose from the aforementioned types. On their website, brief explanations are provided for each structure type. After completing the Articles of Organization (LLC version), one is to then apply for an Employer Identification Number (EIN) through the Internal Revenue Service (discussed in chapter 2). Initially when I applied, I filled in the web form Crystal Morrison/PSYCYOURMIND CONSULTING, LLC. The IRS rejected my application.

Wait, what?

The error message read as follows: *No suffix allowed when completing application.* But, was I not a Limited Liability

Company? Odd. I dropped the LLC suffix and my application was approved within five minutes. Herein lies the difference between the two. I need both a business structure and a tax classification to conduct business. The federal government—in this case, the IRS—viewed me/PsycYourMind Consulting, LLC as a sole proprietor and taxed me as such. The default tax classification for an LLC is sole proprietorship, but I have the ability to adjust my tax classification as I grow in revenue and size. The various tax classifications are as follows:

> Sole Proprietor
> S-Corporation
> B-Corporation
> C-Corporation
> Partnerships

Learn more about these classifications at www.irs.gov. Make sure your state's department of taxation is aware of your tax classification with the IRS to avoid over taxation or incomplete records.

2

There Are No Stupid Questions

Butter

LCPC, LPC, CCM

I am a Licensed Clinical Professional Counselor (LCPC) for
the state of Maryland, a Licensed Professional Counselor in
the Commonwealth of Virginia (LPC), and a board-certified
Case Manager (CCM) through the Commission for Case
Management. This alphabet soup espouses that I am licensed
to practice in the field of counseling at the highest level per
my degree in the assigned jurisdictions. Clinical licensure is
currently a state's endorsement. There is a push for national
licensure to allow clinicians to practice laterally in other states
should they venture away from their original state of licensure.
These licenses further reflect I have completed all educational,

statutory, and practical experience regulations in order to practice. There are other suffixes one may have behind their name. This depends on the path you choose for graduate degree programs. I am not here to argue for or against my chosen path contrasted to others. Choose that which embodies your passion to serve others.

Statutory Requirements

Do you know your state's requirements for practicing counseling? What about the requirements to run a business? Fresh out of graduate school, I had no clue. But as stated before, I have a research background. To quote Will Smith as Christopher Gardner in the *Pursuit of Happyness*, "I'm the type of person that if you ask me a question and I don't know the answer, I'm gonna tell you that I don't know. But I bet you what, I know how to find the answer, and I *will* find the answer." This book is part of my answer.

One thing I would like to posit about grad school; it is a skeleton. Bare minimum. The sheet of papyrus I received after two years of full-time, in-person classes while holding a full-time job, sixty-thousand dollars in tuition debt, and a seven-hundred plus hour combined practicum and internship whispered, "Crystal is teachable." But that's about it.

If you do not embody the wherewithal, intestinal fortitude, tenacity, a get-back-up-again-after-I've-been-knocked-down spirit, you can stop reading here. This book is for those who desire more out of their clinical experience than the degree and letters before and after their birth name. I have had more than one Mack Truck run over my dream than this book can express. Through my experiences, both positive and those which left more to be desired, I hope to show you it can be done.

I received my board certification as a case manager prior to my professional counseling licenses. A stepping stone. I was professionally licensed in the state of Maryland first. Maryland's license to practice counseling is issued by the Department of Health and Mental Hygiene. This license allows me to practice *and* own a business within the same industry. The Commonwealth of Virginia's Board of Counseling was the first state to license professional counselors in the nation. Thus, through a warped elitist standard it seems, their process was (and is still considered by many) a crucible to say the least.

I remember my organization of a Limited Liability Company application for Virginia was not approved until my LPC application was approved by their Board of Counseling.

Checks and balances—the systems communicate and work for the greater good to protect you as the clinician and the prospective client. The clinical licenses are synonymous to business licenses.

During my residency, Virginia required 4,000 hours of post-graduate experience, Maryland 3,000 hours, and the District of Columbia 3,500 hours. These hours are typically completed in no less than two years after your graduate degree has been conferred. They include face-to-face time with individuals in a counseling modality inclusive of individual, group, family, and couples. The hours also include "auxiliary" hours, defined as the administrative time; documentation, scheduling, researching, and planning. These hours, however, do not include supervisory hours.

Required supervision is 100 hours completed in no less than two years. These are direct hours verified by a licensed mental health professional as defined by the state. Due to my license trajectory, fifty of these hours were to be from a Licensed (Clinical) Professional Counselor. Each state has different requirements. For example, Maryland allows an applicant to be supervised by a psychiatric nurse inclusive of other well-known licensed mental health professionals, e.g., psychologist, licensed social worker (LCSW/LICSW), or licensed marriage family therapist (LMFT). The professional designation for supervision provided by a psychiatric nurse is not allowed for Virginia. Ask me how I know. . .

Due to the two-year residency period, these hours seem to be easy to acquire. Let's do the math. There are 52 weeks per year. The average American takes two weeks of vacation per year, leaving 50 weeks in a working year. Fifty hours multiplied by two years equals 100 hours. Numbers do not lie, however, real life does. Take my experience as a cautionary tale.

My residency site was in a private practice setting versus a hospital, outpatient, or community mental health setting. For these reasons, my supervisor was held to a different set of demands and standards than whichever standards she set for herself. With the simple math equation above, it is assumed an hour per week was gained for supervision. Furthermore, I had group supervision once a week with other residents and interns. Great, right? I could double the amount of supervision received and finish in half the time. Wrong! Remember, the states (in my region) mandate these hours are to be completed in *no less than* two years (sometimes three). So, even if I could finish my supervisory hours in 12 to 18 months, I had thousands of face-to-face hours to complete. Of note is how many colleagues and friends I have who finish their

4,000-hour requirement before acquiring all their supervision hours. But wait! How is this possible?

Back to my residency experience. . . My supervisor traveled both professionally and personally about 25% of the year. A week here, a month there. Those absences from the practice began to add up. My colleagues expressed the same sentiment. Not only would I lose one to two hours per week in her absence, my residency completion date drifted farther away.

A few years ago, at a fiscal year start, Virginia reduced their residency hour requirement from 4,000 hours to 3,500 hours. I completed my residency in northern Virginia. At that time, Virginia's Board of Counseling would only accept hours from a residency completed within the Commonwealth's boundaries. Talk about bourgeois! They were the first to license professional counselors, so I curtsy in their presence. The other jurisdictions, Maryland and the District of Columbia, allow hours earned in other states so long as your supervisor is licensed in said state. The supervisory hours are comparable in this region.

Federal Requirements

Internal Revenue Service requires the application of an Employer Identification Number (EIN), which is separate from your Tax Identification Number (TIN), or what most people know as a Social Security Number (SSN). This number is for tax reporting purposes. The application is free and electronic. Visit irs.gov for more information regarding the completion of this application.

I received my number within five minutes of applying. A confirmation letter is also mailed to your selected business address. Do *not* lose the email or hard letter. This number allows you to open bank accounts, transact business as a state vendor, and report income accurately. I have burned several brain cells remembering client details and numbers, but this one is quite important. I have chosen to memorize this number. I am required to enter it for each insurance claim submission. This is how the federal government keeps track of who is paying me and how much. Moreover, my accountant is able to do his thing when my 1099s trickle in from the insurance payors at the first of the year.

Financial

It takes money to make money. In my case, I had to be strategic about where I aimed my $19 per hour residency income—the D.C. Metropolitan area has the fourth highest cost of living in the United States. Before anyone asks why I moved here or why I continue to live here, that's a different book. How I survived *and* thrived during this period is something that continues to surpass my understanding.

Below is a list of the costs associated with the licensure and private practice trajectories. The return on your investment is not always immediate. This career path is regulated in many ways, which creates a time-draining reality at times. Focus on cultivating the investment. Cultivation in this sense is time, money, commitment, and patience.

Articles of Organization for Limited Liability Company (Virginia)	$100
National Counseling Exam	$250
Commission for Case Management Board Certification Exam	$385
Virginia Board of Counseling Licensed Professional Counselor application	$130
Passport Pictures	$15
Priority Postage	$6.55

Maryland Board of Therapists and Counselors Licensed Graduate Professional Counselor application	$75
Maryland Board of Therapists and Counselors Licensed Clinical Professional Counselor application	$100
Virginia Licensed Professional Counselor Renewal (annual)	$135
Maryland Licensed Clinical Professional Counselor Renewal (biennial)	$301
Continuing Education Units (CEUs) average cost per hour	$80
Estimated Quarterly Taxes	% of earned income
Practice Expenses	Discussed in Chapter 3

This profession is not cheap. Not to mention I have expensive taste. I do not have investors patiently awaiting their return in a few years. I started this business with $3.94 in my bank account, living paycheck-to-paycheck. PsycYourMind was truly built from scratch, like my 99-year-old (who will be 100 by the time this book is published) great-grandmother's pound cake.

For those unfamiliar with the word "scratch" and my use of the word, I will provide further detail. This word-phrase means I did not use snap-together components to achieve my outcome. Through trust in God, a supportive husband and family, hard work, patience, discipline, research, flexibility, and more hard work, I was able to establish a thriving practice. This is *my* recipe. Hence, everyone's pound cake does not taste the same.

CAQH

The Council for Affordable Quality Healthcare is a free credentialing database that harbors all things pertaining to practicing as a clinician. The hub then grants access, with your approval, to insurance panels with whom you wish to panel. The verbs "panel" and "credential" are used interchangeably. To become an approved in-network provider is the end-goal of fostering a relationship with insurance organizations. The drawdown of information and application processing takes 90-180 days. More information is discussed below.

NPI

National Provider Identification (NPI) number. Think of this as your professional social security number. However, it is not as sacred since it is asked to be given over the phone frequently. This 10-digit number is free and provided almost immediately after completing the electronically filed application. Visit National Plan and Provider Enumeration System at nppes.cms.hhs.gov for more information regarding the application process. It's utilized for provider identification purposes when calling payors, filling out insurance credentialing applications, and displayed on statements for reimbursement and other fiscal documentation.

Type 1 vs. Type 2

There are two types of National Provider Identification numbers. Type 1 is for an individual provider. Type 2 is for a group provider. Both are free and can be held simultaneously. For example, I have a Type 1 and Type 2 NPI number. Initially, "Crystal Joseph, LPC" was registered for Type 1. However, due to a convoluted brokerage system in health care, and a misunderstanding by this system of my sole proprietorship, I was required to apply for a Type 2 NPI, which I currently do not use. The Type 2 was mandated because of my use of the business name PsycYourMind Consulting, LLC. Should I hire any employees, I will then have to utilize my Type 2 NPI number to reflect the permutations of a group practice.

Medicaid Number

Medicaid is allocated per state. Thus, I applied to the Medicaid system in which state I chose to practice (Maryland). I have yet to apply to Virginia's system, as the process is quite different. Remember, I have to curtsy in their presence. This application is lengthy and requires your undivided attention to ensure no mistakes are made. I submitted a paper application. The approval process takes approximately 60-120 days. Medicaid requires a renewal and upload of licenses biennially upon renewal with the state board. This is an electronic process. If you do not upload your renewed license, Medicaid will kick you out of their system, and any claims you submit will not be reimbursed. It is as if you don't exist. Ask me how I know.

Currently, in the state of Maryland, Licensed Graduate Professional Counselors (LGPCs), which are pre-licensed professionals, are not allowed to provide therapy in a private practice setting to clients who are utilizing Medicaid as their insurance. I spoke with the policy representative to gain clarification. Per her report, pre-licensed professionals may provide therapy to clients who are utilizing Medicaid in an Outpatient Mental Health Clinic (OMHC) due to the facility holding the license, and therein having particular staffing requirements—psychiatrist, nurse practitioner, etc.

My reply to her was this: The psychiatrists and nurse practitioners are not directly supervising the LGPCs; that is the job of the LCPC, LCSW or clinical director who may hold a PsyD or PhD. This means I am not allowed to provide oversight to an LGPC as a licensed therapist when I would sign off on the notes and provide direct supervision???

Her response was firm and reflective of the regulations set forth reporting, stating Medicaid reimbursement procedures follow the license; the OMHC is a licensed facility whereas I am a licensed individual. Word on the street is my colleagues are seeking change of such regulations. I, too, am concerned pre-licensed individuals would not have a chance to be confronted by intersections in the therapeutic forum from those whom hold state insurance, such as Medicaid, unless they have experience in a community mental health or OMHC setting prior to venturing into private practice.

Authorizations

A form that authorizes psychotherapeutic services for a specific amount of time. Maryland Medicaid utilizes the term "units." Once eligibility of coverage is verified, an authorization must be completed. Maryland Medicaid will typically authorize twelve units at the outset. Viewed synonymously with the number of weekly sessions, I could see a client for approximately three months. Once this authorization is exhausted, claims will not be reimbursed. I repeat: You. Will. Not. Get. Paid. Thus, you, a billing specialist or credentialing specialist, must stay atop of how many units a client has remaining. A lot to keep track of, right?

I exhausted an authorization in my naivety of starting my practice. Steady submitting claims week after week. Then I checked my bank account. Um, where are my ducats? Frantically, I called Value Options (formerly Beacon Health). I explained my greenness to the representative on the phone. She was gracious enough to walk me through the process of reauthorizing. This justification of services generates a new authorization with 24 units and is good for six months. Wipes brow. The rejected claims can be resubmitted; however, the return of payment can take up to 30 days to process.

Vendor ID

Once credentialed as a Medicaid provider, registration with the payor's clearinghouse or broker of payment (currently Value Options) is necessary. Visit valueoptions.com for more information on applying as a vendor. A clearinghouse is a middleman who transacts data and moves money, in this case, on behalf of the authorizing entity (Maryland Medicaid). Value Options was previously Beacon Health. As if a therapist did not have enough to worry about, you now must keep up with company buyouts and mergers, as well as policy changes associated with such transactions!

I spoke with a representative at Value Options to clarify their role; Value Options is actually the payor of services operating as a broker, if you will, and not a clearinghouse. For example, PaySpan (www.payspan.com) could be considered a clearinghouse. They shift money from payor to payee. Bank account information, vendor ID, and NPI number(s) are needed to set up this account.

Once your application is approved, a vendor identification number is assigned, which corresponds to claim remittance data. Remittance is a formal word for payment. This can be tricky, as this number corresponds with your *servicing* address, which may be different from your *mailing* address, which may be different from the address you registered your business under. Heed my warning: Should you change locations after becoming a Medicaid provider, notify both the state Medicaid office *and* the payor's clearinghouse.

THERE ARE NO STUPID QUESTIONS

Your vendor identification number will then change. Should you submit claims via an old vendor identification number. . . You. Will. Not. Be. Reimbursed.

CEUs

Continuing Education Units. Accumulation of these hours are necessary to renew your license annually or biennially. The number of hours required is dictated by the licensing board or other statutory requirements. These units, in some cases, must reflect a competency domain as well. A competency domain is one set forth by statutory regulations and encompasses a knowledge area. For example, professional development, cultural competency, and ethics are all competency domains for the Boards of Counseling in Maryland and Virginia.

Private Pay

Otherwise known as fee-for-service. The arbitrary, competitive and comparable price set forth by clinicians for services. The more special and rare the clinician, the likelihood a client will pay a higher fee. This higher fee reflects an investment of self, versus a cookie cutter service. Below is a graphic representation of my initial revenue structure. The proportionality is synonymous to how I sustained myself for the first year in business.

Three tiers remain as I enter year three, however, the ordering has changed. Maryland Medicaid clients were the bulk of my clientele—you see, this is my base and largest tier.

While Maryland Medicaid has the lowest reimbursement rates of the insurance and managed care organizations, which I currently am a provider for, the reimbursements provided a steady income for many reasons, one of which included the need of the population, particularly those members searching for a non-outpatient mental health clinic (OMHC) environment. The other weighted factor was due to the cultural background of those holding this insurance type in my region. The history of the patient's mental health experiences, or lack thereof, which led to their help-seeking behaviors beyond what is "given" to them by the system is discussed in *Conversation with a Clinician of Color: Likeness, Lucy & Lemonade*.

I have heard both colleagues and clients state their disgruntlement with the Medicaid system. Colleagues feel it's a waste of their time or the clientele can be "difficult." Moreover, clients have an arduous task of locating practitioners who are not employed in an OMHC environment. To date, I have had more issues with Carefirst than I have with being a Maryland Medicaid provider.

My second tier was made up of members who held

traditional insurance benefits of the likes of Carefirst, Cigna, and the list goes on. This tier was reflective of my working-class and middle to upper-class clientele who also have my evening session times on lock. Many of the Maryland Medicaid members can come during the day due to under-employment, unemployment, or status as a student. The traditional insurance members typically work 9-to-5s and can only see me after 6:00 p.m., given the traffic and unreliable public transit system.

My top and smallest tier during the first year were private, self-paying clients. These clients pay my declared hourly rate and have flexibility in their schedules. Some come during the day; others come after work. My self-paying clients do not use their financial freedom to snub others; many choose this form of payment for privacy reasons. When someone throws down their insurance card as a form of payment, I am required to submit the claim with a mental health diagnosis from the *International Statistical Classification of Diseases and Related Health Problems, Tenth edition*, even for the "worried well." It is assumed we as therapists drive private pay to pad our pockets. It's quite the opposite actually—we are ethically required to do no harm.

Figure 1. PsycYourMind First-Year Revenue Structure

Paneling/Credentialing

The process by which one is invited, certified, and regarded as a provider of services for a managed care organization or insurance body. This process can take anywhere from 90-180 days. My suggestion is to hire what is known as a credentialing specialist. This process must be navigated with vigor, and your vigor belongs mostly to your clients or building the practice. See the resource list at the end of this book for these professionals. Yes, you have to spend more money—their expertise is not free! Mistakes cost money, at times, more than you have. I was able to complete my Maryland Medicaid, CIGNA, and Carefirst applications on my own, but hiring a credentialing specialist would have saved me time . . . time I could have been spending making money

The credentialing applications are lengthy and may require additional information to be submitted incrementally. There are times when a particular insurance company does not have any more room to add on providers. For example, Aetna, a highly used insurance company in my region, is not accepting providers at this time. For this reason, I cannot serve clients with this insurance. Clients have also transitioned after open enrollment season or a job change, as I am not credentialed with Aetna.

3

Stay Ready
Eggs

*"Eggs play an important role in baked goods.
Eggs add structure, leavening, color, and flavor
to cakes. It's the balance between eggs and
flour that helps provide the height and texture of many baked goods. It's a balancing
act." –Joy the Baker (October 28, 2013)*

Let us go back to my time in grad school. Second year. Practicum complete; knee-deep in my internship. Below was my
Tuesday and Thursday schedule.

6:30 AM	Wake up . . . but not really get out of the bed
8:00 AM	Leave the house
8:28 AM	The time I really left the house
8:27-9:44 AM	Viciously navigate Route 1; I-295; the Key Bridge; MacArthur Blvd. (horn blown 5x) No pedestrians or cyclists harmed during this daily commute.
9:45 AM	Scan for parking in Tenleytown; circle the block; whip Nadia (my car) into a parallel spot as if Paul Walker trained me.
9:52 AM	Run across the street . . . don't buy heels you can't run in, ladies!
10:00 AM	Morning meeting
12:00 PM-5:00 PM	Case management clients . . . I drove to them. To all the smart people who asked above at 8:27 AM, "Why didn't she just take the metro?" This is why.
6:00 PM	Fight for parking on K Street (parking garage $20, out by 10:00 PM) or street parking. Decisions, decisions! Budget? What budget?!
7:00 PM-9:50 PM	Class (work on-call phone ringing during lecture)
10:30 PM	"Home again, home again. Jiggity jig."
11:30PM	Contemplate life . . . I pray it won't always be like this.

My schedule on Mondays, Wednesday and Fridays went something like this:

8:45 AM	Seven-minute commute to internship site. Bless God!
9:00 AM	Morning meeting
9:30 AM-3:30 PM	Groups/Individual sessions/Supervision
3:30-4:30 PM	Notes
5:00 PM	Home
6:00-10:00 PM	Homework
11:30 PM	Did I eat today?

My week equated to almost 80 hours of go, go, go. During one particular one-on-one meeting, my internship supervisor noted despondency oozing from my pores. I verbally unloaded my daily routine, passion for therapy, why rainbows need unicorns, and where they manufacture glitter (whoever "they" are). He was quite respectful in touching upon the things I felt I "should" and "must" and "have" to do in a given 24-hour period. I mean, we can't all be Beyoncé. Tuh!

He challenged me with this: "Crystal, you were clearly made for this, but I wonder if you're running on high octane, if not diesel." I scoffed. He continued, "At this rate, you will burnout before you even earn your degree."

Through appropriate self-disclosure (which was important to model to me during this learning period), he explained the intricacies of his work-life balance as a father, psychologist, and program director for a community mental health agency. I was "responsive to his feedback," but . . . (BUT negates the nonrestrictive clause or participle phrase prior to the comma—thank you, Ms. Brown and Ms. Purdy).

How many times have you heard, "You have to work ten times as hard to be just as good"? So, frankly, when would I ever be allowed the privilege of having balance if I wanted to be great . . . or even good?

Per Joy the Baker's quote, I lacked leavening, structure, and texture as an intern. I had enough flavor, though (#BlackGirlMagic). In my head, I knew I was better than good. I was (am) great. Tony the Tiger. But (nothing to negate here) I was going to have to let some things go.

Homework versus dishes. Hair versus practicing a presentation. I have natural hair, and most recently completed a second big chop to make room for administrator-type, 50,000-foot altitude responsibilities. Hair is work. Short or long. Straight or coiled. Time is money. And in this case, I had to trade my vanity for time.

"No" versus "Yes."

Someone once told me, "No is a complete sentence." I was in awe of this. It is the subject, the predicate, and the punctuation. There is nothing more potent than "no." Wait . . . yes there is. The look from two pews ahead at a 38-degree angle from a woman who is not your mother, yet will tell your mother you were acting up in church. That is pure saturation. So, I had to employ saying "no." Behaving "no." Loving "no."

My job function mandates my senses, mind, and heart for the people who seek my services. People who are hurting, wondering, wandering, questioning, and *being* in this thing we call life; I am a servant to them. I cannot take care of them until I take care of myself. This meant (and still means) saying "NO." There were so many times in the past when I wanted to say "yes." I'm sure in the future the same will apply. Learning to employ this small word with so much power has helped in my balancing act. I've earned the aforementioned privilege by saying "no."

Psychology is a science. My colleagues and I are teased by those in the chemistry, physics, and biology industries that it is not a hard science. If your brain stops working, can we then talk about how hard of a science psychology really is? Insert "OOOH" gif. You know the one. . .

I can build a circuit if that helps anyone questioning my

practical scientific nerdiness. One that works. Daddy's girl. Ever wonder why we have light switches? Perhaps not, or you don't care. In order for electricity to travel, the circuit must be closed. When the light switch is on, the circuit is closed. Conversely, when the light switch is off, the circuit is open. I use this premise to provide structure and leavening in my day-to-day schedule.

When I'm in the office, my clients have my undivided attention. Phone is on do-not-disturb. Oh, you didn't show up within the 15-minute window, let's reschedule. "Hi, my 6:00 p.m. didn't show, would you like to come earlier? Okay. Great. See you soon."

After I lock my office and unlock my car, it's 57-minutes of "Bootyhopscotch" radio. Don't judge me. The PsycYour-Mind switch is off. A new switch is turned on. Attention to detail. Time management. Logistics. Balance. I earned the name "Big sis logist" from my childhood best friends. This is why. I suppose I possessed what I needed to begin to balance out all that flour (vision and creativity) I mentioned in the first chapter.

I soon realized I can still be Tony the Tiger great, elicit my magic, get seven-to-eight hours of sleep, have my hair behave, and not have my friends side-eyeing me if I can't attend their events without overexerting myself. As I've said before, though, this right here (insert relieved exhale) has taken practice, failures, attempts, risks, "I-told-you-so's", tears, laughs, a forest of trees in applications, the Philatelic catalogue of stamps, a $0.38 bank-account-balance-trying-to-pay-to-get-out-of-a-hospital-parking-garage, trust in God, trust in man, trust in no one, and trust in myself.

One of my favorite childhood books is Dr. Seuss' *Green Eggs and Ham*. Sam-I-Am entreats an unnamed character to try green eggs and ham. Say it with me: "I do not like them, Sam-I-Am, I do not like green eggs and ham." Nostalgia. The moral I gather from this story is, don't knock it until you have tried it, even if it looks weird.

I remember whining, "They didn't teach us business in grad school." "I don't know how to do this." "I'm scared I will lose money." "What if no one shows up?" "I do not like private practice Husband-I-Am." Because going into business for myself looked weird!

One of the BIGGEST lessons I've learned so far on this journey is you will never know unless you try. I humbly implore, please try. Whatever it is. One's fear threshold increases with age. The permutations of our environment become predictable. We fear the unknown, because "Wait-a-minute, I didn't predict that." Thus, we stay in our comfort zone.

Eggs are the structural provision flour needs. Texture is the lasting characteristic. I was not growing in my comfort zone; flour gains no texture without eggs. Earning my texture was important. Texture defines my weight in gold in proportion to the other ingredients needed to remain empowered during this business venture.

I guess I do like green eggs and ham.

Location

I was once told, when purchasing property, the domains to assess are safety, niceness (curb appeal), and affordability. It was also said in the same breath that only two of the three domains can be held. Pfffffffffhhh. I like to believe I have all three when it comes to my office location. I feel safe, and per the report of my clients, they do too. I have a wall of windows, which allows natural light to permeate, and an unparalleled view of evening sunsets.

My mother's bequeathing of 120-inch silk drapes did not hurt either. I pay $400 per month for 400 square feet with a shared common area. Utilities are included, a steal in this area. And, before anyone asks, yes, the landlord is responsive.

As I have grown and continue to grow, this low

overhead cost allows me to practice and live below my means in order to retain my income. Pay attention to surrounding development where you wish to locate your practice. I have some background working for a real estate attorney; my husband is an architect and urban designer/developer. If you do not have access to this knowledge, consult a professional (listed in resource appendix). I locked in my lease for two years to prevent outside real estate comparisons from driving my rent up as the surface of the community changes around the building. The development in Montgomery County is spotty. This is due to stringent building permitting regulations and costs associated with development.

4

Find Your Voice, Then Crank up the Volume
Sugar

Sugar has the unique ability to heighten flavor or depress the perception of other flavors. Recent studies have also denoted the addictive properties of sugar. For the purpose of this book, I will leverage the addictive property as a flavor heightening property. Of course, too much of a good thing is unhealthy.

As you have noted, I have not sugarcoated my experience. I want to make it plain so you hear me. Loud. And clear. Making a private practice from scratch has been a challenging, yet enjoyable experience. I have learned a great deal about myself during this process. One thing is to crank up the volume.

In my teens and early twenties, I was more gangsta rap

than gospel streaming through Bose speakers with bass on 3.5 and treble on 5. After the death of my dad, during my junior year of college, I lost much of my volume. I am working on cranking up my volume while equalizing my "sweetness." This sweetness is power, fortitude, and strength. The volume of sweetness is meant to depress weakness, mediocrity, and inexperience. While carving this path, I have learned people are intrigued by my experience. I developed mentorship, internship, and residency programs as a result. For my colleagues, professional peer consultation is also available.

An incident happened after graduation which caused me to reevaluate my decibel level. Eager to begin the application process to become a Licensed Professional Counselor for the Commonwealth of Virginia, I sent off a 5-pound priority box of course syllabi, the licensure fee, and application itself November 2015. Three months later I had not heard back. I submitted an inquiry of my application status. I received a vague letter stating my application would not be accepted. What do you mean, it will *not* be accepted?! Furious, I threw not one, but several tantrums. My two-year's worth of blood, sweat, tears, sacrifices, financial stress, and health was denied by the Board of Counseling in Virginia. Not to mention I maintained a 3.8 GPA while going to class from 7pm through

10pm, holding a full-job, and helping my baby sister with her homework. Their "no" was the equivalent to hearing "what you've worked toward is not good enough." I inquired why. Another vague response. Infuriated, yet again I went to the Facebook group for recent graduates. I posted a picture of the rejection letter and wrote "has this happened to anyone before?"

I did this at the top of my lunch break. By the time I was biting into my apple while walking back to the office, I had a missed call and an email from the Dean of The Chicago School of Professional Psychology. She told me to take my posted letter down immediately from the Facebook group or I would be blocked from the group. Furthermore, she posed if I did not take the letter down it would prevent her from helping me resolve the deficiencies listed in the letter. Wait, pause. Did she just tell me to take it down or else? Was this a threat? How could she threaten me for something I paid for, let alone earned? Moreover, I had every right to consult with other students who matriculated through this institution after being sold a dream licensure attainment is guaranteed in the D.C. metropolitan area. Rolls eyes. This would be the first of many power plays I would have to bow down to in my journey to obtain licensure. I just didn't know it yet.

Resourceful and still annoyed, I consulted with an

attorney. Boards of counseling follow bureaucratic standards which are issued through regulations; codes of law and ethics based on the state. My situation escalated above my pay grade and I needed someone to guide me who was not biased, nor frustrated. We met twice. In our two meetings he proposed two directions: One, I sue the school with a class action suit against false advertisement of guaranteed licensure post-graduation; or two, I work with the Dean to resolve the deficiencies. Should the deficiencies not be successfully resolved, he would represent me during what Virginia's Board of Counseling calls an Informal Conference. Don't let the adjective of "informal" draw the wool over your eyes. After consulting those who have come before me, this *is* a formal hearing. Think, "Please state your name for the record."

I partnered with the Dean and we were able to produce a resolution to the Board. They needed a list of full faculty to evaluate the standards of my education. This was a sticky situation because my campus was new, a satellite location for the well-known Chicago location. The faculty who taught me were not all full faculty, some were visiting or assistant professors. Was it possible the Board was questioning the school's integrity as well? The resolution document was forwarded to the board spring 2015.

Radio silence.

I inquired two more times the status of my application. It is November 2015. I reached out to my Virginia State senator. Virginia's Board of Counseling falls under governance of the state. I explained my grievance at length. Virginia had declared several states of emergency regarding mental health during that time, yet like many other applications, mine was held hostage to an antiquated and staunch system. He reached out to the licensing director on my behalf to inquire of the status. Please note, I participate in local, state and federal elections. I am no stranger to my representatives. I am blessed he heard my disappointment to act on my behalf. Within two weeks, I received an apology letter from the executive director of the Board and a promise my application would be reviewed in full. This is why the Board and I are on a first name basis.

It is now January 2016. I received my license to practice in Maryland by Maryland's Department of Health and Mental Hygiene, Board of Professional Counselors and Therapists. Still no sign of Virginia's approval. Y'all I'm tired. Then on a November 2016 evening, almost a year later, I receive my approval. Too tired to smile to laugh to rejoice, I cried. Tears of relief. Find your voice, then crank up the volume. Even if it is uncomfortable. For the volume will be heard by others walking the same path as you. Your voice, the louder it is, macerates the negativity. I will continue to advocate with volume and sweetness. This cautionary tale amongst others is why I am passionate about mentorship, internship and residency programs within the counseling industry. It does not have to be this hard. Hear me please, it does not.

Mentorship

> *"Not having heard something is not as good*
> *as having heard it; having heard it is not as*
> *good as having seen it; having seen it is not*
> *as good as knowing it; knowing it is not as*
> *good as putting it into practice." -Xunzi*

A mentor is an experienced lay leader or professional who can provide guidance for the mentee's goals, interests, and passion. A mentor is also available to the mentee to provide support on an ongoing basis. Mentors may also assist mentees with other networking opportunities relevant to their professional career.

A mentee is someone who is interested in developing an ongoing relationship with a more seasoned lay leader or professional who can guide him/her/them on their volunteer path within an organization. Mentees may also be seeking additional networking outlets for professional development.

Internship

PsycYourMind has three internships per year—spring, summer, and fall. It is an eight to ten-hour per week paid program. Available to bachelor and master-level students with educational backgrounds in psychology, counseling, social work or a related field. PsycYourMind is an approved internship site for the Undergraduate Psychology Department of the University of Maryland. If you are interested in refining your clinical skills or learning more about the private practice experience, I encourage you to apply for an internship in your area.

Residency

Residency is a post masters-level, paid experience. Denotations are as follows: Licensed Graduate Professional Counselor in Maryland; Resident in Counseling in Virginia. Accrual of indirect and direct hours. Supervision provided.

A listing of board-approved supervisors is located on your State Board's websites. Visit mdbnc.md.gov or dhp.virginia.gov for more information. Approval to begin a residency is required from the State Board with an extensive verification process before onboarding can occur. Passing of the National Counseling Exam is necessary for Maryland. Residents must hold an unencumbered professional liability policy.

Approved Clinical Supervisor

I am an Approved Clinical Supervisor in the State of Maryland. This means I can supervise Licensed Graduate Professional Counselors (LGPCs). In some instances, my license and this endorsement allows me to supervise other provisionally licensed mental health professionals (e.g., graduate marriage and family therapists). However, the bulk of an LGPC's supervision should come from an LCPC. Through this professional designation, I serve those aspiring to become licensed mental health professionals. I do not want others to make the same mistakes I did to become avid advocates and leaders within this field.

5

Accept Your Humanness
Vanilla

The role of vanilla in sweet baked goods is like the role of salt on the savory side: it enhances all the other flavors in the recipe.

Contracts

Read. Interpret. Ask. Do NOT sign anything you are uncertain of. Let another person lay eyes on those words. And by another person, I mean an attorney or accountant. Here's my cautionary tale. Poses in Slick Rick fashion for this story. I was given a contract that held the guise of a sublease. It *appeared* suitable. Remember, I've worked for several attorneys in my other life. I have experience with reading and interpreting contracts. Or so I thought. Within the contract was the following clause:

> *"Contractor will pay 40% of the first $3,000 and 30% of $3001-$6000, and 10% of additional total payments received by clients to cover the Rental Fee. This includes payments for the use of facility, utilities, electronic health record software, marketing services, and other costs associated with facility rental and administrative services."*

At first glance, this appears to benefit both parties. I interpreted the percentages of payment to encourage my growth in business. Finite increments of payments based on tiers, separate from each other. Until it was brought to my attention I was interpreting the clause incorrectly. I thought rent would be $800 for grossing $2900 in one month, which is partially correct. However, once I reached tier 2 ($3001-$6000) and tier 3 (+$6000), I owed a combined percentage. Instead, when I did reach tier 2, I was paying *only* 30% of my income and not the combined 40% of the first $3000 earned, which in turn benefited *my* growth, as assumed earlier, and not the landlord's.

I was told with disdain I was paying incorrectly *after* the contract lapsed. I consulted my attorney. Thank God for her! Her research proved this contract was unethical and illegal. I was stunned. Hurt. Heart in my butt. I was writing $1,500 checks for 100-square feet (with no windows) when I could have leased my own three-office suite! Comps in the area for an office this size with similar amenities were no more than $650. To add insult to injury, I discovered my white counterparts did not have the same contractual rental agreement. In fact, their rent was less and not indicative of a tiered percentage rate. And no, my landlord was not white. So here I was, a black woman, serving as a wet nurse to nourish someone else's greed.

I was emotionally abused and threatened by the landlord once my attorney advised them of the breach of ethical and legal nuances within the contract. We eventually reached a settlement, but not before being called out my name in public. Meekness is strength under control. I had *a lot* of control that day. Thank you, Jesus! I have worked too hard for the letters behind my name. I reminded myself of who I was and whose I am.

I consulted the police to escort my husband and me to get my personal belongings and furniture out of the office the day I elected to move out. I did not want to put myself or my husband in a position where it was our word against the landlord's. Or a black man's against the landlord's. Because #BlackLivesMatter.

For every adult, one police officer is required per the corporal I spoke with serving in Maryland. Thus, three officers showed up on move out day, unbeknownst to the landlord. I did not file a formal report. The bodycams and my body remember. My menstrual cycle came early due to stress. I was tearful. I felt sheepish. I was reminded of my vanilla—my enhancement of everything around me. How others cannot go where I go. How I had a waitlist after nine months. And to never *ever* (cue Trillville) let someone bring me down when I'm doing right by me and mine. If you ever see the aforementioned verbiage in a contract. Run.

Integrity, Mission, Value

Protect your heart. Protect your character. Protect your reputation, for this precedes you in time. A boundary is postulated to exist between the personal and professional with regards to self-disclosure in session, of course. However, with me, what you see is what you get. Sitting on a pew or in front of my clients, at lunch with my girls, or on travel for business.

My personal is political and professional. I'm one and the same. Yes, I turn switches off when leaving my office to go to a social event. The point is: make no compromises. To paraphrase Maya Angelou: People remember how you made them feel, not what you said.

To my earlier reference in chapter one; the investor fired me. Let me go with no formal paperwork. To make matters worse, I, to this day, have no idea why. I have deduced the following: my immediate supervisor threw me under the bus.

Has this ever happened to you? Someone feels threatened, perhaps? It was assumed I had another job, which was unwelcomed per the terms of my employment agreement. I did not have another job. One day, I happened to be dressed up to head to a date with my fiancé (now husband) directly after a meeting with my supervisor. I remember she continued to compliment me and ask where I was going. None. Of. Her. Business.

Another issue was that she was unqualified to supervise me per Maryland's Board evaluation. The Board instructed me to pose a query to my employer about options to be supervised once I obtained my provisional license as an LGPC.

Remember the white paper for which I served as the research assistant and subject matter expert? You guessed it!

The exact bibliography I constructed, totaling six months of research, was published with no authorship mention of yours truly. I still have the original document saved. At this point, I was tired. Not angry, just tired. Tired of being used and seen as expendable. The plight of the Black woman. Educated, Black woman. Viewed as a threat, not an asset. Or was I only hired for grant funding, tokenism, or maybe the ill-applied diversity definition?

I know, I know. You're probably wondering why I did not take legal action. By the time I was notified of the printing of the white paper, I was six months into my residency. I did not have time for political and legal permutations. PsycYourMind was an unrecognized seed, and I needed its mere potential more than I needed a fight.

When I learned how to drive, Mrs. Uzzle said, "Integrity is using your left turn signal to change lanes at 2:00 a.m. when no one else is on the road." Guess who uses their turn signal at 2:00 a.m.? Not just on the road, but behind the closed doors of my home and business. The mission of PoundCake & Private Practice is to teach by showing, improve by doing, and inform by explaining. My values are reflective of my upbringing and experience. I have circumscribed along my personal and professional journeys.

Consulting Services–Know Your Worth

The saying goes, "Know your worth, then add tax." I conducted professional trainings prior to acquiring my licenses. Teaching runs in my blood thanks to my great-grandmother, grandmother, and great aunt. Dynamism as a business owner is necessary. Because I am my service, burnout is inevitable, yet preventable. I must position myself to have my services make money for me even when I'm not present. This requires a steadfast phasing model and the right people around you as the next facet is cut. Not only am I a licensed therapist, I am also an approved sponsor of continuing education, an author, an approved clinical supervisor, and the list goes on. These facets all generate money. Some require me to be in the room, while others do not. Keep this in mind as you grow.

Do not burn your bridges, as you never know when you will return. As you refine your skills, state your worth to those who wish to consult with you. Do not negotiate. Do not back down.

Niche

African-Americans. Black folk. African Diaspora. Anxiety. Depression. Cultural Trauma. Racial Identity Development. Define your niche. Maintain the skills and education needed.

Educate others. My niche arose out of a deficit. I had the education—double psych and Black Studies major. I had the experience—Black woman. I have the training—10 years in the business. Consider your strengths in clinical practice. Assess your weaknesses or least favorite clinical presentation. Work toward becoming strong in all facets of practice. This includes assessment, diagnosis, written advocacy, treatment plans, community infiltration, and cultural competence.

Outcomes

"Outcomes" is a buzzword used in the industry to denote tangible progress, change, or modification after the direct application of an approved intervention. It is the child of evidence-based practices. However, some of these so-called evidence-based practices are not normed to populations of color. (Insert niche here.) With experiential knowledge and a research background, I am able to maintain adjusted outcomes with my clientele. My interventions are tailored using the needle and thread of cultural competence and social justice.

Billing

Learn the permutations. Know how thy coins cometh and where they goeth. Then, when you are comfortable, hire a billing specialist. I am speaking from my experience. Your preemptive billing experience and acknowledgement of your own budget serves as a fiduciary control. When you decide to hire a billing specialist, an expectation has been set based on the realities of how your business is run.

My billing specialist knows when my claim reports are due, so much so that she now reminds me if I forget to send them in by Saturday afternoon. Claims are reimbursed at the rate they clear the portal. Not at the rate at which you submit them. I detected payment within three-five business days. However, during open enrollment period and the turn of the New Year, claim reimbursements were processed over a two-week period. Which brings me to my next topic.

Live Beneath Your Means

Save for a rainy day, for rain will come. A storm will too. I am a shoe lover. Love of shoes. Do I own a pair of Louboutin's? Not yet. Notice, I didn't say "No." (Stares off into the distance.) That $695 (or reduced eBay rate of $295) is better put aside for second-quarter taxes. Or used to leverage a second-office location in Virginia. To quote Jay-Z: "Wanna know what's more important than throwin' away money at the strip club? Credit." Even though I have not completed a loan application, my credit and savings accounts were used to determine my worthiness to lease a commercial space, and will continue to be utilized as I grow. Just because you have a high credit allowance, does not mean you *have* to use it, blow it, or flaunt it.

I recognize my business is like a two-year-old in age and temperament. In need of changes of clothes in case there is an accident, and extra food choices due to the picky palette. I wouldn't give a two-year-old a marker and expect coloring outside the lines not to occur. Same can be said for what I am able to manage and maintain three years into owning a private practice. I do not say this to place limits on myself, but to be realistic about discipline needed.

I love the thrift stores in the D.C. Metropolitan area, and have no shame about shopping there. I wash my clothes just like the next person. Pray away the spirits. I walk out the house looking fly every day. My favorite finds so far include a Hermès Roi de Soleil scarf for $2.98, which retails for $300, and a Louis Vuitton (French Luggage Company authorization) Josephine wallet for $12.99, which retails for $400. For this reason, I have coins to push toward business growth, personal goals, and more money than month left. If hard-pressed, I can sell my high-end items for added capital.

Overhead Fees

Decide how much you can afford. Affordability includes mistakes, hiccups, and no-shows. Ask yourself the following questions: Are utilities included in the lease agreement? If not, are they averaged amongst the tenants in the building? An office in a large building will look differently than leasing an office in a smaller building if this is a factor. Business internet and phone service costs more than a residential account. Bundling discounts may be available should you use the same provider as your residential account.

Is there onsite parking? Will you have to pay for parking or public transportation to get to your office?

Marketing is a must. Do you need business cards? Should you update your LinkedIn account or other online profiles? Should you hire a public relations specialist or social media strategist? As you grow, your reach will also. Allocate enough funds for digital marketing, directories, and, of course, the traditional business card or promotional pen.

For your salary, are you paying yourself via dividends, or are you stroking a check biweekly? Consult an accountant and tax attorney for further explanation. Will you have employees or contractors? How long can you support your workers should an insurance contract be dissolved or claims not be reimbursed? All these things must be considered when assessing cash flow, revenue, and startup costs.

No-Shows/Error of Variance

I am in the business of people. To serve them even when they choose not to be served. There will always be no-shows or impromptu cancellations. The planned cancellations can also put a dent in earned per diem. Thus, I have calculated my gross error of variance.

I schedule 16-20 clients per week. By Thursday, the last day of my workweek, there are approximately two cancellations. For the month, my error of variance fluctuates between eight and ten percent. Then there are those weeks everyone shows up, giving your brain a run for its money. Expect these weeks to occur after a major event (e.g., school shooting; election), around the holidays, and as the seasons change.

Many private practitioners like myself have no-show fees and cancellation policies to protect our time and the business. I've driven an hour to the office only to find the client, who I came to see, canceled via email while I was en route. Not only was their session time not better used by someone else, my time, gas, and wear and tear on my vehicle went down the drain.

Typically, I use this unscheduled time for resource development, administrative tasks, or to post on Instagram. I note the error of variance decreases when my ideal clients are sitting across from me. They are willing to put in the work to promote wellness on a weekly basis.

ACCEPT YOUR HUMANNESS

6

The Oven

Can't stand the heat? Get out the kitchen.

Want to start a private practice? Scared you'll fail? Worried about meeting unsavory people wanting to take advantage of your naivety? Let me help you, help you. *PoundCake and Private Practice* serves as a recapitulation of lessons learned. Continuing education unit workshops, professional peer consultation, as well as internship and residency programs are available to assist you further on your clinical journey.

The continuing education unit workshop is six hours of professional development. This workshop meets three of four Maryland Department of Health and Mental Hygiene's qualifications: (1) Maintain professional competency; (2) increase professional knowledge and skills; and, (3) prepare for new roles and responsibilities in the practice of counseling or therapy. Participants will progress through modules designed to enhance knowledge in order to prevent deficiencies in clinical practice and entrepreneurial roles.

Peer professional consultation is for those who wish to touch base about a difficult case, teach work-life balance skills, or to learn of statutory requirements after relocation. And, as these pages note, graduate school programs are unable to teach everything needed to run a successful practice. From theoretical applications, to culturally successful interventions, to celebrating the little things, the internship and residency programs facilitate a flexible learning environment while providing clinical structure.

PsycYourMind internships facilitated through PoundCake & Private Practice are paid. The internships are for Bachelor and Master-level students wishing to augment research foundations with practical application of theory in real-world situations.

From year-one to year-two's end, I tripled my revenue. My accountants and I were pleasantly surprised. The recipe? A leap of faith, determination, refinement, and a need within my identified niche. When I set out to make PsycYourMind, my credit was not "good enough" to apply for a small-business loan. I did not have a business mentor. Student loans were and still are the devil. I was not married. All I had was my vision, questions with not enough answers, preparedness from prior external provocations, voice (at a low decibel), and my humanness. With these five ingredients, I was able to start, make, and now maintain a thriving private practice. Not, of course, without heat and time. At times, I pinch myself. Dreams really do come true.

Reflections

I would like to thank the following people and businesses who have supported, assisted, cheered me on, and snatched my edges when necessary:

Jesus & God—because without either, I am nothing. Thank you for my gifts and listening to my whispers.

Daddy—I got the worm. My nickels and dimes aren't adding up as much as they used to. I've accepted my nature, even when it is not my intention. Until we meet again.

Fabrice—Thank you for reading between my lines. For holding true to our vows, even though they did not include entrepreneurship. Love you.

Mommy, Amani, Tobias, and Jordan—The apples do not fall far from the tree. Mommy, thank you for being steadfast no matter how thin the air was on the high road. For mastering the art of sublime. Amani . . . ahem, Dr. Morrison, thank you for being better than my Barbie dolls. Tobias, thank you for our phone calls while I drove an hour home from my residency. Jordan, thank you for always finding the humor in life and your gathering efforts. Love y'all.

Naisha and Michelle—Thank you for raising the man of my life. Thank you for supporting me through fashion, food, and fellowship. I love you all.

cBNJ™—Twenty years of friendship. Britt, thank you for showing me twerking and loving God is acceptable. Noey, thank you for the curbs and Skittles conversations. My hair is not where I said it would be, but it is safe to say we made it! Jam, thank you for being the turn-up Queen and giving the best directions on the backroads. Love you all.

Laura—Roomie for life. Thank you for your continued support and understanding. William & Mary excellence.

Nubia, Ashley, Bai—All the shade, all the laughs, and all the encouragement. Thank you

Shyla—Thank you for telling me I could be the plug and believing it. Thank you for sharing some of your electricity in this process.

MinGlen, Bishop and Pastor Nat—Thank you for my spiritual foundations in Christ, and for always giving me a platform over the past twenty-three years.

My clients—Thank you to those I've served, and whom trusted me in their journey to wellness.

Those wishing to climb—I see you. Thank you for the encouragement through your desire to learn.

TCSPP Tribe—Thank you for continued support professionally and personally.

Janine—Thank you for recognizing my skillset before I did. Thank you for helping me refine it with your sunshine.

Margo—Thank you for my PsycYourMind logo cookies, which never last more than 15 minutes. William & Mary Black excellence.

Rashod—Thank you for laying the digital foundations for PsycYourMind and teaching me how to do backdoor maintenance.

Shé—Thank you for picking up the ball and helping me phase and build PoundCake & Private Practice. William & Mary Black excellence.

Nicole—Thank you for the cover layout and design.

Tyrone and Shane—Thank you for the cover photo and being there for our major life events.

Stephanie—Thank you for keeping me out of trouble. William & Mary Black excellence.

Larry and Terreon—Thank you for keeping my ducats in order, and providing encouragement for new entrepreneurs. William & Mary Black excellence.

Tearanie Parker—Thank you for helping me see into the future and plan accordingly.

Brandon—Thank you for digitizing the PsycYourMind logo.

Guarav on Etsy—Thank you for the PoundCake & Private Practice logo.

Sarah Kosterlitz, Inaugural PYM Intern—Best. Intern. Ever.

Shivonne, Dr. Alicia, Dr. Joy—Thank you for truly living by #CommunityOverCompetition. Shivonne thank you for being my clinical accountability partner. Dr. Alicia thank you for being earthly confirmation of this project. Dr. Joy, thank you for the creation of Therapy for Black Girls, a national directory of Black therapists who serves Black women, girls, and men.

Priyanka—Thank you for submitting my claims.

Joylynn Ross—Thank you for your graciousness in editing my book with flair and semblance.

DC Community Printing—Thank you for producing quality marketing and educational print materials each and every time.

Maryland Family Resource, Inc.— Thank you for allowing me to hold the first "Absorption of All Colors" training in your facility, and being the premier agency who serves families and children in Prince George's County, Maryland.

Industrial Bank—Thank you for your commitment to our community, and being the premier Black-owned bank in the D.C. Metropolitan area.

And to all the experiences that made me a better woman, clinician and colleague. . . Thank you.

CRYSTAL JOSEPH

Resources

Clinical

Therapy for Black Girls by Dr. Joy Harden Bradford
Therapist Directory & Podcast
TherapyforBlackGirls.com

Therapy for Black Men by Vladimire Calixte
Therapist Directory
TherapyforBlackMen.org

Akoma Counseling Concepts
Shivonne Odom, LCPC, LPC, NCC
Akomacounselingconcepts.com

Help Me Hodge
Dr. Alicia Hodge
Helpmehodge.com

Financial

PC Financial Services, LLC
Larry Pendleton & Terreon Conyers

Funding an Empire
Tearanie Parker

Legal

SKT Legal
Stephanie Thomas, Esq.
James W. Backus, Attorney, P.C.

Social Media & Web

#AskAsh Consulting
Ashley Shuler

Sushe Design
Shé Langley

TheRebelSociety
Rashod Harris

About The Author

Crystal Joseph is a Licensed Clinical Professional Counselor for the state of Maryland, and Licensed Professional Counselor for the Commonwealth of Virginia . . . or what most people call a therapist. Crystal is certified as a case manager, sponsor of continuing education units, as well as an approved clinical supervisor. She is the owner of PsycYourMind, a thriving private practice in Silver Spring, Maryland.

Crystal received her Master of Arts in Counseling Psychology from The Chicago School of Professional Psychology, and Bachelor of Arts in Developmental Psychology and Black Studies from the College of William and Mary. Crystal is the author of *Conversation with A Clinician of Color: Likeness, Lucy & Lemonade*, a clinical, first-person commentary peppered with research and pop culture.

Adept in honoring the diverse backgrounds and cultural beliefs in the therapeutic setting, Crystal partners with adolescents and adults. Her interventions are outfitted with pop culture, media, and world event references as appropriate.

Crystal's love for research afforded her the opportunity to partner with Georgetown University's department of psychiatry as a subject matter expert in the development of a white paper on case management. She is a volunteer of the Disaster Mental Health function of the American Red Cross for the National Capitol region, and helped with the historic flood in Louisiana, August 2016. When not in session, you can find Crystal cooking with cast iron, or curating her shoe collection. She resides in the D.C. Metropolitan area with her supportive husband, Fabrice, and teacup Yorkie, Lyric.

Learn more about Crystal at
www.poundcakeandprivatepractice.com
www.psycyourmind.com